FLIGHT SONGS

Notes for an Album of Exile and Rebirth

poems by

Stacey C. Johnson

Finishing Line Press
Georgetown, Kentucky

FLIGHT SONGS

Notes for an Album of Exile and Rebirth

It is impossible to grieve in the first-person singular. We always grieve for someone and with someone. Grieving connects us in ways that are subtly and candidly material. I am not yet sure which group I should join, where to envision myself, on whose shoulder to cry.
—Cristina Rivera Garza

America, I do not call your name without hope.
—Pablo Neruda

What if the cosmological constant is not just particular but anti and ante-particular?
—Fred Moten

ACKNOWLEDGMENTS

For displaced people everywhere, and all lives and spirits of the earth.

In defiance of the killing machines of empire.

Poems in this collection appear in The Inflectionist Review, Ginosko, Open
Skies Quarterly, Silver Rose Magazine, Cosmic Double, and Brushfire
Literature and Arts Journal. I am grateful to the editors of these journals.

With special gratitude for Leah Huete de Maines and Christen Kincaid for
ushering this book into the world.

Publisher: Leah Huete de Maines
Editor: Christen Kincaid
Cover Art: Mark Wade
Author Photo: Mick McMurray
Cover Design: Elizabeth Maines McCleavy

Order online: www.finishinglinepress.com
also available on amazon.com

Author inquiries and mail orders:
Finishing Line Press
PO Box 1626
Georgetown, Kentucky 40324
USA

Contents

An Invocation

If I am to be severed from my first attachments, make me a bridge between relief and this emerging specter.

Let me accept what may follow this request, including instructions for rooting this body as an anchor in what it dreads—or else I am no link, just a floating possibility.

Let me brace against what may yet be, extending out over the dark deep, to this unknown shore: the craggy, silty, boggy knot of its broiling terror.

Lend courage to this limb, that I may hold. If I am far from the tree, let my spine be the crossing from the land of none to the place where it might yet be.

Once

. . . To be torn apart
is my ambition,
            not, like Actaeon, limb
by limb, but in a prolonged waltz
of changes, every measure a new
            hiding place opening up
within me . . .

            —*Wayne Koestenbaum, "Shéhérazade"*

THESE NUMBERED DAYS

Mon
A body can go three minutes without air, as many hours without shelter,
as many days without water and weeks without food, and everything we
knew was an incomplete list. We carried like our packs a sense of keeping
something. It was watch.

Tues
Holding minutes without air against hours without shelter, we sat with things
beside us, newsfeeding our screens and everything we could know was a list
we couldn't carry.

Wed
Still unfinished, it was mostly ads for credit cards. We sat with things beside
us, patrolling the feeds of our screens. We were sometimes killed by them,
woke up anyway—remembering against the possibility of extinction, our
inventories of need.

Thurs
Checking our roofs, we were only killing sometimes and recalled how when
we woke. We were meaning to watch the mothers, trace the gas lines meant
to call them back from their escapes.

Fri
We bored the rifles, safed the locks, but who would watch the babies? We
checked drums for the water to save us, called them back, they escaped
across our rifles, we locked the safe, shined.

Sat
The drums: would there be singing? We forgot, and in the dark times we had
numbered and yes, we said, for the living.

Sun
—and the dead, we would be keening loud about our dreaming ends.

HOMELAND

The breaking was tremendous. All we could say
in our silences was all we knew of this descending
dark. Our flames burned like the dendrites we lit
when we touched in forbidden spaces in the days
when space itself was forbidden—except when you
were claiming, making, owning, taking it, and we
were twirling tiny leotarded dancers in the wind.
We would not go gently, we whispered, refugees
from ourselves, from the forever metals and the
concrete that no one would name except when
they were about to be paved.

We laid hands into its give, as if to take it back
and heal what was choking beneath it, as if to say,
Look. That was me, I was here, and the roles were
forever ambiguous: the hero or the damned, the sailor
or the slaughtered, the seventh son or the seventh daughter
in a row buried up to her neck for seven days in the heat,
learning to wait.

My people are not the ones to tell you how to think, and I
spent lifetimes wishing they were but we are fluent in the
language of losing it all, and if you cry wherever two of us
are gathered, you will not be alone, we will listen with you
to the wailing in the wind of the mothers on the road making
the sounds of their babies after they stopped.

Our voices are what we raise because we have found no other
way yet, to call attention to those forever without them,
who died without—

We were listening and the war was everywhere,
but so was the noise and it rose
a B-movie zombie
grabbing our necks.

TORN SKY UMBRELLA

I stand as witness to the common lot
survivor of that time, that place.
—Anna Akhmatova

All of us were implicated.[1]
This was the grief of our age, to
wake inside the belly of the whale.

Still, we sang songs of absolution.
These were for Jonah, now mute
with fear, and for the babies.

For the babies, it was a womb
we might sing away
from the grave.

---

1 A Note on Epigenetics: We wanted to birth *The Waste Land* or the *Cantos*, but our people were not the sort to grasp allusions to most figures of antiquity. We carried its deaths in the milks of our breasts and in the seeds we erupted when we came, and we were always coming, always looking.

We were the peoples that were stranded on the craggy shores, holding babies starving against hearts while the land's lords feasted on Good Friday steaks.

Without access to capital-H histories or capital-P publishers; without a seven-digit following or five good reasons to do—anything, we can offer you only this record of how it looked when we were looking, during a prolonged moment at the ends of our ancestries and some beginning not yet named.

HOLDING PATTERNS

We travel on the surface, in the expanse, weaving out imaginary
structures and not filling up the voids of a science, but rather,
as we go along, removing boxes that are too full so that in the end
we can imagine infinite volumes.
—Édouard Glissant

We baked bread and held the babies.
We remembered bread and babies,
sat in parked cars, shook our heads,
wondering about others behind glass,
shaking heads, and at those walking
in circles in the intersections, waving
arms to shout. We could not decipher
them yet

we looked often to the creatures nearby,
kept them close in our homes, in our cars,
in our beds we studied their movements
and tried to read their eyes and faces, we
gave food and names, followed them with
cameras, listened as to ciphers and kept
watch, as with oracles. They were judging
us, we knew. But how?

The children looked away and talked less,
and outside play we once took as birthright
became fraught as religion, history, and plans.
Everywhere you looked, there were images
over images, and they held us.

Most of what we did was wait and watch.
We'll see, but it was a question. See? Maybe.
We watched the sky and bread, the ovens, and
the pets, watching us, and the children, there
was something we wanted to tell them. Wait,
we wanted to call to the children,

the right words. It was silent except
for the noise, which was everywhere,
like the next beginning about to erupt
from the holes of our mouths.

THAT YOU MAY NOT BE BITTER, ANGEL

May the sky that tears with every imminent coming wrap you
still in its infinities, barely contained. May you notice the webs
noiselessly repaired in the shade-giving tree.

Hold the noise that shatters you, not the first to turn your ears
to the hush of leaves against leavings, breaking clouds in chorus
with hawk, *You!* and then into drums of our bellies, roiling trees.
Know as above, so—Watch dancers, a single amoeba and each
their own, the leavings remembered in chorus over the grounds
where they keep our unnamed dead.

May you see a low bird on a long branch, while violence sways
its blood-red breast[1] leaning to hear the wind even when
the answer is another sword to pierce the next heaven.
When you know what this is because flesh won't forget,
swaying eulogy in concert with the still uncounted,
we'll wait for you here, beneath our torn heavens,
to find your next sign and trace it.

May you cry, holding the line when the time is right,
stitching these wounded forevers, cut from your stolen crowns
to the ties they axed for the tyrants who meant to prevent its return.
Sky ripples after the knife in a ribbon of sound, what were we
looking for except a means to ask if we still meant
to rip ourselves—

Out from what, exactly, she wanted to know,
and from the seams above us and she shook
our dead, reminding, *Child, did I teach you nothing?*

Arms up, *Up!*

---

1 Swaying, but holding. May you better hear these drums as songs our time and distances
and dynasties of death would have killed had they not perceived alone and in chorus, how
sight in the days of our division comes from holding what still moves, to ask, holding still,
what moves?

NEITHER FLESH NOR SPIRIT

When they came for the silence of our sacred,
hiding weapons behind badges, the guards,
by way of greeting, shouted *Speed!*
planting flags in the flesh of our flesh.

Waking from sedation, we took them
saying, *Mine!* and rarely *Out!*
After that, movement meant aggravating
wounds. A body learns to stay, shouting.

Here I am! Forget the still, small voice.
We thought at first of walking to one
another on woven stories, but the guards
searched our song in the wind.

They blocked that, too—for a time, anyway.
Trespass of the mind became a punishable
offense. Consider concrete and a moving
substance—how it alters the
        path.
        The shape of a river changes.
      You
         get
            wind
                tunnels.
                The dammed river
                becomes a reservoir,
                its former trajectory a wasteland.
                Now what?

The living will move.
What this does to memory
remains, as the saying goes,
to be seen. We looked and listened.
Hands reached and bones breathed.
There was a whisper beneath the gale,
saying, *Rise.* No one was watching,
and we heard.

TAKE IT, BUT NOT FOR THE TAKING

Amid some immediate grief,
one pose involves the adoption
of wrappings and funeral attire
for cinematic effect, leaving
with a full plate of food
and dry eyes.

Or you could remove
the bandages beginning
with your own in order
to lay the wound before
another and wait bleeding
head bowed raw against
unknown elements.

Leave the funeral
hungry.
Then the body.
Visit the waiting grave.
Notice its size and shape
fit for your child
your whole life.

Now try giving it back
keeping only what
you cannot explain
and notice the everything
there. Find it in you.
Try again: head bowed
eyes closed ears open
as your hands. Knowing
that your borrowed clothes
may outlast
your borrowed skin
offer anyway:
Take it. Say it again
and now wait.

FIRST LESSONS IN FOREVER TIME

Ignorant of possibilities for landing,
we flung fire and broken bones
into unwritten star charts.

Sister, you offered creation to them fresh again,
undressed wonder at the findings you already
knew, hearing as they spoke of light

A beaming face to sky past the watching
stars not-yet-lit until—a child, they raised her
body, shaking, *Look!* and always up.

What do you see? you asked her, below
the freeway hush, crows scraping air into concrete
above, she pointed, blurring probabilities of decay.

They said *Wait,*
and they say the sea people on ships were first invisible
with no knowns to frame their image, but you learned
like making a fist upon waking, to wait until the grip
takes in the difference between can and will, spinning

between poles
of now
and had
once been—

     once

         between chaos and our becoming

Later, it was canned stew in the desert and
gas station spoons, a process of learning what causes
meant to men. You grew your own called *Hang On.*

You learned to recognize ships like any other
weather, when shadows stretched and purpled dark before
stars erupted like fists punching to the whole light
on the other side of a paper sky.

NOTES BETWEEN CAGES

If a scream erupts in a burning forest of old growth
unknowns and no one—
>   stops, what do you call the ensuing tug toward old growth
>   flight?

If a bird in the hand is worth two in the mouth
but the mouth is gagged—

>   did the species in question forget its song? If the cage is un-clocked but
>   the door still closed are its captives free? Is it time?

A body will do what it will until met by an opposing force.
Except with protection of children—

>   If a light shines onto eyes shut tight has anybody witnessed?

And can I get one?
>   Now?

If you build a dam across a river and the river is time, what do you call
the resulting body?

>   Is it a reservoir? What have you saved. And for when?

These eyes trained on sky still guide wild flights by stars, set courses for
migration at midnight—

>   But what can they find in the glow bleeding from empire cities?

Still singing hallelujahs of *nobody knows*, forever-present notes that
know what no hand grants, no thief can steal.

Reaching back to the original promise in the first split of atom from an
original rib to give birth to the genesis of song—

>   In the space of a womb, this surrogate tomb for the still unburied,
>   long dead still—
singing unnamed solids behind these gates
the liquid river sings us—

>   still

singing our—
>   home.

BALL HURLED HIGH

Morning steam against our black hillsides,
through carcasses of former homes
we counted losses like it meant we
might keep—

something sought supplies while it
emerged lumps in the chest, soft tissue
spots on our tongues our sex at the backs of
our throats we washed these

—our reflections, and they watched
us for the next betrayal in the time
of leaving these times, they said

rooted bodies also reached, but
what for? For to burn scatter hope
for a soft landing and rain

on the slope above the river, mama
with the girl in the ash, telling risen
lives, unfolding one. And one, pocket
recipes from a time when meals rang,
bells before the blasts broke
          the rhythm there were fire poppies,
birds of ash, cleansing torch and the fire
it rained us down.

Confessions scattered back ash
from the urn against the wind, we
stick tongues and lick cremains,
chalk-slick sliding into another tale,
the great light broken it scattered
invisible flames, tiny and forever
on the verge of gone
—this is why you look
she said to find the missing
we held up songs
she said to call

          them

                    back

FLAME THROWERS: A RETROSPECTIVE

Remember when we shot our breaths out of ourselves, laughing
at the last loud blast? We couldn't stop and we sprayed gasping
iridescent drops into the air like water from the spray nozzle of a
garden hose, just for dancing.

We played chase like being hunted was a game, like capture was a
cartoon scene, we fell, laughing. *Wait*, we said, *I need to catch*—like
it was slow feathers falling from the sky to be cupped in our open
hands—And remember, how we painted with it, too?

We blew our canvasses across car windows, fingertips tracing: here
a smile, now a cat, heart.

And sometimes it was smacked from us, as when we fell back
off a ladder or a swing, but the trick to waiting was knowing the
metaphor and trusting that if the next breath could be knocked out
like a ball from a basket, it could also come swishing back at the
next run up the court, catching nothing but the nets of our wide-
stretched throats.

We didn't think about squandering, then, and it never once
occurred to us to save any of what we spent so freely, those
fortunes that we took for our inheritance.

We had no way of knowing, then, how easily they could go. Really,
it takes only a certain amount of pressure, applied across a certain
length of time, but how could we have begun to measure what we
had yet to grow the strength to apply?

We couldn't, not when time was what we flew through, roaring our
laughs like lions until they ran

out

Then

Let me tell you what the sea does
to those who live by it first it shrinks then it
hardens and simplifies and half-buries us
and sometimes you find us shivering in museums
with tilted feet so that all we can do is lie flat
our colorful suffering faces watered away
we who threw fish lines into these waves and steadied our weight in
mastless long boats
and breathed in and out the very winds that wrecked us

—Alice Oswald, *Nobody*

CLEAVAGE

We wait beneath our windows, hunting for bodies of light
along points of fracture because old women told us
it was once whole.

This before it cracks from our seeming solids
in the dark, whereafter: everywhere we look,
there we are, in pieces.

Palms behind us tremble shadows across carpet
past our feet and the racket of the voices we absorb,
those parties of projections, leaking to and from.

After the cries stop, we hold our gaze. The eyes
are tricksters, the ears are, too. We resist the racket
of voices in the rooms without furniture.

We hear less when we need to, dulling senses
quiet through the storm, hacking mattress into
the eye that echoes what we once did.

Pressing hard into our unclean flesh, unwashed
and put away, we hear him leave, out to sail
the desert boat he'll die in, hard and buoyant.

We hold our unclean flesh in piles on carpet
where he leaves what he meant to build
before the fires and floods, and this hunger.

Amid cold, heat and the rising cicadas,
coming to harvest a song in concert with
all he has been meaning to do while counting

piles of things he still wants to need in the end.
He labels, but never the water except to wash,
and he puts them away, marked; the closet is full

and still he sits, piling boxes by the porch, shadow
of palm running over our toes until his back is so full
that talk turns to fault lines beneath the lake of dead fish.

Filling the closet, he dreams of the desert he keeps
meaning to lose himself in, its shadows in the carpet
at our toes and we watch them, and him, through the
bright of noon dead filling the rooms we meant to hold
still by looking sideways into the blur of our pieces,
blinding us out of sight.

FORKS IN THE CRYING ROAD[1]

When I put my hands on your body on your flesh, I feel the history
of that body. Not just the beginning of its forming in that distant
lake, but all the way beyond its ending...
    —David Wojnarowicz

From the peak beside   the cellphone towers
We watched you in your   cars and on the street.
You moved in lines and   waited; eyes glazed with blue light
over asphalt and concrete, breathing in fumes.

We watched you in your   cars, over the street.
The noise was endless, and you couldn't hear us
over asphalt and concrete you breathed in fumes.
In lines and waiting, you were listless and deaf.

In lines and waiting, we   said to you:

Enter   here.

---

1 **A Note on Certain Customs Relevant to this Image**: "The Crying Road" is also known as the Via Dolorosa, or way of grief. Some context: It is customary to murder the liberator to protect the orders of control from infection by the designated dangerous, who tend to earn such labels by their willingness to free—

It was nothing, it was an act that could be avoided by allegiance to the bond between right and law, might and awe—and silence, above all. Him they loved he held the woman they meant to stone, so the tribe of the sons of Adam long twisted by appetites for tender flesh long lusted to defile every Eden had their way in a dark hour.

They pierced the body, blade into torso and he bled like a woman in silence, stripped and mocked, another eaten dog in the land of relentless opportunity.

FREE THOUGHT IN CAGED TERRITORIES

In the land of perpetual   progress, the only way
to die is by   choice, and each new attack
submits its   proof of provocation. The machine
needed fuel: our blood, but the tank was hidden.
Those who looked   cried out or were sentenced
as long as the   heretics were locked away, everything
was smooth as   the surface of the mirror world,
now the beginning   and now the end.

In the deep, whales bled.   What are you aiming for here?
The machine's precision   was its aim. Targets sighted
without eyes stripped   and mocked; efficient to enhance speed.
Archangels crawled   on the blood-slick floor of the temple
before the veil was   split to beg for bread though
our lips were   sealed the angels whispered
to the floor and   only those at the mop
could hear[1] them   and the dying.

---

1 You, unhearing, could not know   how we wanted you to see against the fumes.
What would you say if you knew   to answer   instead

of waiting for us to come   in the dark against the fumes, crying over steering wheels,
shadowed beneath buildings?   If you knew, how would you answer, how we would watch
witness to the whole   in your hunger, and call again, *Look   up!*

The ants marched one   by one and over nailed beams; things went on,

quietly occurring.   Someone fed the mouths, silenced cries, so we picked them up
hungry, from our   cages no one heard but the winged at the mops who reminded
us here to remind them   beyond their mirrors so they built new limbos in the desert
to hold us like the   goats of Leviticus, we carried the sins of the tribe we held them
on the land in our mouths   sewn shut.

WEEP NOT

When you met the women,
you said

what kind of	*Daughters hea*r and we understood
look to those still	company we kept, and someone said
before the gas	with eyes and we held them open
of the murdered	it burned our witness and the mothers
we heard them	sons of men kept on beneath the helicopters
on like the	and the megaphones they kept
after the babies	keening women on the silent road
	and

we followed on   the road, after—[1]

the babies

---

1 **Aftermath**: As the babies were losing their cries, the keening women gathered them to chests to gallop them over hills past the shadowed valley, the snipers at the gates. What else would a dragon keep but these against theft of treasures it could not know the golden virgins: the pose of the hour was vigilance against the useless piles, and it curled at our ankles, holding us to their warnings against loss.

The eyes of the witnesses were burning, and through tiny speakers in our ears, the guards at the gate said go home, and the curators of spectacle insisted, there's nothing and only the crazy

and the sentenced kept on and the angels at the floor with the mops, and the dead.

Open casket equals	open door to enter the theater of mourning
then came hawks	and the hawkers went the blind
mice Now run,	someone said, and we did then
the farmer's wife.	Admission was free to the public,
see how they—	

History was removed by the surgeons. They held efficient needles to our lips, we were the crimes against their progress to be sentenced, but our eyes were burning from the gas, and our faces wet you fell three times along
the road and we with you   the guards feared.

KISS THE BRIDE

The wolves are in the garden now
and guards have built a church.

Circling and thirsty for the blood
of our lambs robed men
become pets to the men seeking new wools,
for insulation against the chill wind.

The wind carries a common cry
the opposite of silence
daring opposition, to their deaths
like bodies screaming
to be washed. They knew song
the site of least resistance.

Gears turned dust across
the graves our lady
wept.[1]

---

1 **Look like a mother**: Ever after, these pietàs continued to loop over our memories of sons and how his first sounds were not words and the sermon sighed back to the crumbling mount, *you will know them in the end*—bodies again, and draw tiny fingertip sweeps from the edges of their eyes to the bottoms of their chins to wonder about those fingers, always. There in the mirrors you would not name always and everywhere as if the only thing that mattered was the reflection of light back your cries would stop above their wheels salt across your faces, we watched your sunrise break from them, shouting, *Look!* from this peak above the city, beside these towers. Veils off, now come.

NOTES FOR AN EXODUS

once
We rehearse our only testimonies, coming soon,
and castles fall away from our foundations
like ozone from atmosphere, babies from baskets,
holy from firm, our castles fall away[1]

until our bodies become the make-believe of TV
merchants, babies in snow among palms; in packs
across the valley, in avocado groves freezing outside
the angel city, among the make-believe.

Wildflower bodies after wet winters in bags demand skies
be tested, and they testify on speculation, spewing relative
reports, but we know along the road beneath the blades,
what is and is not clean.[2]

then
Cities flood past news; the anchors will not hold. We wave
from rooftops again across Broadway in john boats, bloated
bodies of old pets in hallways, floating. We can't keep up.[3]

Floods recede, mold advances. Heads announce plans
to rebuild. Our figures irrelevant, the waters of our eyes'
tides rise seas, militias, prophets, cults—all pressures

Trying time against time our waking dreams
we do not breathe but cough
the wind's departing hush and—

---

1 Our windshields ice over, birds fall from the sky, the angels collect our bodies in bags, probing
waves of speculation catch on camera our faces iced over; we fall, and they swear sprouting
theories: we can only speculate.

2 We light a candle for the driver who swerves from our flocks after a party like wildflower
bodies in winter in bags along the road our purple feathers pool in gasoline the crumbling way
to our castles, coming soon.

3 What is the latest count—for which disaster? Excess of numbers makes numbers irrelevant.
Our eyes water through leaking boats. Aftermath stories scripted at breakneck, our necks
breaking to keep up.

after
Bodies of ours   float. Rising, we still—

We recede, give up plans for living, take capsules in the morning
and move on. We lock the doors, forget insurance—again.

We hang on and amid the hangings,

we let go, dropping reins keeping time
and come the morning we forget, until
our seeds burst against our locked pins
of light, our fists loaded with pollen spores

fleeting shivers against time
our waking dreams and salt
between our lips
flats on our backs
bursting the flowers
on our lips   we locked our faces
into the stars in our skulls, still

Rising, we still—

---

4 We still against a moving voice. Now come.

After

My love is for the ocean,
But since I—a bird
Must be excluded from the deep
I haunt the solitary shore and weep.

—Faridud-Din Attar, *The Conference of the Birds*

WADING IN

The babies wanted to know if it was time. It didn't matter
for what. We were always telling them to wait.
They thought time meant the opposite of waiting.
And then what? A boat can only sail so far on a lake
of dead fish, with the flies like clouds and the womb
of our voices warming coffee in the backs of our songs
in the beginnings of our voices, the places behind our
gagged silence, which endured against the hands of
the holders, nearing the edges of our breath where they
could no longer seize[1] it, coming.

---

1 Which is not to say they didn't try, but we knew better knots for the roughest seas, and
we know to practice our ties even in moments of becoming and especially now, as we pass
our histories across tables and channels, in exchange for crude maps.

Where to? Some knowing, we hope but will not say. We name instead our somewheres,
each seeming distinct.
What pains us now is knowing none of us can ever arrive—anywhere or ever—except
with these others. Strangers, each seeming bound to separate yesterdays amid crossings,
re-crossings, these inherited meanings intended with such

density		we can hardly
move anywhere		before
one or another		of our limbs
are caught again		in our nets
and we are forever		stopping
over these	knots.	

Eventually, we give ourselves up to the net and it wraps us in ties. We drop sails and
surrender to moving by nothing but current and whatever binds us in silence, hoping it
familiar.

FROM RUBBLE

After we've read and re-read
the last bomb-shelter bedtime
story, enough that we no longer
need the books, after the skins
of our backs have collectively
dulled the barbs at our borders,
after children no longer know
the difference between fire and
sky, what will we know for
certain, except the common
ghosts? Floating among
us like pigeon feathers.

When the rags of our bodies
are strewn across the singed lands
of our erased ancestors, and we've
burned the last of our vengeances
in the name of the justices we stood
before rights, when the mute children
no longer need to be hushed,
will we remember to offer
a beginning in our next

word?[1]

---

1 Like a balloon, they say, when they hear these mammals singing, deliberate in
dismissal of the possibility that what is loosed here is an admonition. They consider
it a mandate to avoid all reference to a common soul, especially regarding these
familiar lamentations they can't say we are naming ourselves, renaming us in our
own image. They can't speak of our ambitions, buried wishes, furtive wonder,
clandestine griefs. They can no sooner detect these than remember what happened
in the age of flowering plants when forests stretched pole to pole everywhere the
shallow seas when we splashed a chorus laughing, before the lines of our bodies
separated at the forked branch in the palm of our last common mother, as if to
prophesy those glorious calamities that would make one of us forget this common
womb. What did you think, we call when you noticed we would not live for you in
captivity? One, listening, observes: We are here, and finally hearing, holds.

TRUTH AND RECONCILIATION

I am taking back what I said about the flesh,
before I felt the teeth of this machine. Return
to my breath, placenta, let me dig what graves
may come in time. Don't touch me
forever. These cameras grope[1]

Terminal announcements come quick, *who do
you think? You are* and now the doings wonder
what? Think. Anything unattended in the terror
will be removed by our security until you answer.
Join these contents in chorus, out! I'm keeping
the body, take my voice. Watch the tent as it tears.
This is the belly and I am the whale.

Kick now, Jonah. Do you think this time among us
was ever but in question? Let old vows reappear
by this remaking while another womb confronts us.
Ancient beginning, speak.

      We

              are

---

1 Considering the screens and their little mirrors. We were taught not to mention
it, not to look the forever look. How much the face! But to lose it, I tell you, is not
so bad. I would have done it sooner if I knew. Not to make light of the ones that are
eaten by chimpanzee, by thrown acid, by the temper of a man punctuating outbursts
with gunfire—only of the weight they carry, our obsessions, how they fail our blind
unseeing, always thinking it knows. Take Moses and the face of God, and God like,
No but wait and I will show you my backside, as if to say, it's not my face you want,
trust me, and there I go again, still coming back to the lesson, which is nothing but
the face of knowing.

Our faces were veils to be lifted, presenting us brides to the unknown which was
everything after they left.
The waters in the lagoon, now
look   now   reflection now
the canyon, looking back   now the tomorrows

on the eve of our births.

Grieve, sister. This is what
you do unto we.

cont...

CARRYING

I carried the babies on the road
when they were wailing
and you carried me when I stopped
and there came nothing
coming to take us by the black in our
eyes and you met us there, singing.
There, you said, you will come
and join me here. Sister, remember how
we carried our new languages to sleep?
You had a wand and you turned it upside-
down
and all the moons and stars floated to the
top, again and again, and we floated with
them, stardust, starstuff, it was all of us
and it would be another ten years and a
missing
home before we knew it, after we had lost
our first sentences and the lights of our
bedroom
play, and fractured into dialects of our own
and neither really knew what the other said
or where to begin learning, it's no wonder
and it was all of wonder, that we were always
trying to see.

Consider the mirror effect,
how they must have been looking at you,
at us, just as hard, and how hard we
tried to pretend that we had not attended
one another's births in those moments
of heart-play, in the dark, as I lay
me down, we whispered, meaning not to
sleep, instead played foreplay
to our mutual becomings, and in the
heat we lay in bed in star-patterned
underwear with bare chests, and I asked
you to run your wand across my skin,
barely touching, silent and secret as
a prayer   I carried your blame
baby where you dropped it, and you
played the fairy in my play. I asked
you to say the lines I gave your mouth and
filmed you giving yourself, over and over
again, and now I see you in the kitchen
at the stove, and you say to me
sister

Sister, you say to me, try

27

the only answer
remembering the tunnel
on the road where we left

this
and you place it on my tongue
my full mouth
of our cries and the babies

their first words.

BAPTISM

We sang each other's names.
It burned our eyes
to look against the gas and
now was the time
for our tears. Machines
gnarled the earth and the flesh
of our flesh with metal
teeth and the bones sang
between them, refusing to be
swallowed again. Louder, we
said, louder now.

FLIGHT SONGS

We pulled the husks of cicadas from our ears
and the buried songs emerged from these
gestating skeletons, and in the end
we held them, dusting toward our lives.

Unless a grain of wheat falls to the earth
—and we pulled the husks of cicadas from
our ears—and dies, so that the buried
songs emerged from our forthcoming
bones

unless we pulled the husks of our
songs from our ears as we died,
we could not sing, we could not fly

unless the buried songs emerged
from the dust of the husks of
our bodies, from the ashes of
our once and future wings.

Notes

Once

Cristina Rivera Garza's work consistently underscores the central place of the land's dead, and the importance of honoring the way that literature develops in community. Of special relevance here is *Grieving: Dispatches from a Wounded Country* (translated by Sarah Booker, The Feminist Press, 2020).

"Homeland" (and related poems in this series) are in conversation with David Wojnarowicz's lament, "I am fearful of something more than fear: it's something in the landscape . . . something out there that feels so empty, and it is not made of earth or muscle or fur; it's like a pocket of death with no form . . . I feel like my soul and my flesh will suddenly and abruptly be consumed within the civilizational landscape or else expelled off the face of the earth" (*Close to the Knives: A Memoir of Disintegration,* 39)

> *also*
> Images of crying on the road, carrying babies, as applied to migrants anywhere, have been particularly central to my imagination since reading David Lloyd's vivid depiction of the keening of the Irish mothers who carried their starving babies during The Hunger. My first encounter with Lloyd's work (which is extensive on this topic) is "The Memory of Hunger." (in *Loss: The Politics of Mourning,* Ed David L Eng and David Kazanjian, University of California Press, 2008.)

> Reference to zombies is inspired by the work of Henry Giroux, specifically *Zombie Politics and Culture in the Age of Casino Capitalism* (Peter Lang Publishing, 2011) and *The Violence of Organized Forgetting: Thinking Beyond America's Disimagination Machine* (City Light Books, 2014).

"Under a Torn Sky" includes an epigraph from Anna Akhmatova's "Requiem" (written between 1935 and 1961 in response to the Soviet Great Terror) and also responds to philosopher Timothy Morton's comparison of contemporary ecological awareness to that of the Biblical Jonah finding himself inside the belly of the whale (in *Dark Ecology, Hyperobjects,* and throughout Morton's work).

"A Note on Epigenetics" takes inspiration from the work of Dr. Rachel Yehuda on the biological and spiritual manifestations of intergenerational trauma.

"Holding Patterns" includes an epigraph from by Édouard Glissant's *Poetics of Relation.* Glissant's work is a consistent beacon of hope for possibility of transformation of collective dislocation (Trans. Betsy Wing, University of

Michigan Press, 1997).

"Neither Flesh Nor Spirit" nods to Bob Marley's statement, in a widely anthologized 1979 interview he gave to Vivien Goldman: "I don't believe in death, neither in flesh nor in spirit."

"Take It, But Not for the Taking" is informed by the gospels and contextualized by Cristina Rivera Garza's *The Restless Dead: Necrowriting and Disappropriation* (translated by Robin Myers, Vanderbilt University Press, 2020).

"A Ball Hurled High" borrows from Salman Rushdie's observation, "The exile is a ball hurled high into the air" (*The Satanic Verses*).

Then
Religious imagery in this text is deeply influenced by the work of David Wojnarowicz, especially *A Fire in My Belly*. My first encounter with his art was in 2018 in the context of Dr. Yetta Howard's class on censorship at San Diego State University, where the heart of this collection first emerged.

Specific Wojnarowicz texts of interest are the artist's memoir *Close to the Knives: A Memoir of Disintegration* (Vintage, 1991) as well as letters, interviews, and other records presented by Cynthia Carr in *Fire in the Belly: The Life and Times of David Wojnarowicz* (Bloomsbury, 2012).

Wojnarowicz considers the mechanics of silencing in his essay "In the Shadow of the American Dream: Soon All This Will be Picturesque Ruins" (*Close to the Knives: A Memoir of Disintegration*).

David Lloyd characterizes this silence as "the violent sealing of an empty, howling mouth" and stresses the responsibility of the living to counter this silence, for "if even out dead are not safe from us, the enemy will have won" (Eng and Kazanjian 205-228).

In *Humane Insight: Looking at Images of African American Suffering and Death*, Courtney Baker asks, "Did the sermon die when the Mount crumbled?" Baker's work explores the education that involves a "collapsing, a falling of the self into the reality of the other" (x). Her work informs the "Crying Road" imagery that dominates this section (University of Illinois Press, 2014).

In *Grieving: Dispatches from a Wounded Country* (also featured under "Once"), Garza writes, "We moved from town to town. . . knowing that we carried a border with us. This knowledge, which is a treasure, is also a place of birth."

After
The footnote below "Rubble" originally appeared as "Indiri Song" on *Breadcrumbs: The Unknowing Project* and was inspired by Sam Jones' 2021 article "Madagascar's Got Talent: Lemurs That Sing with Rhythm" from the Science pages of *The New York Times* (25 Oct. 2021).

"Wading In" and "Baptism" respond to the call of the classic spiritual, "Wade in the Water," which was invoked as code by Harriet Tubman and others in the underground railroad. Howard Thurman draws strong parallels between the passage through metaphorical troubled waters into the redemptive promise of biblical texts.

"Flight Songs" is in conversation with these lines by Matsuo Bashō: "Nothing in the cry of cicadas suggests they are about to die."
Also, with the *Gospel of John*: "Unless a grain of wheat falls into the earth and dies, it remains alone; but if it dies, it bears much fruit" (12:24, *English Standard Version*). Also, with imagery from Victor Serge's "Hands" particularly as expressed in these lines: *Am I alone . . ./ Or are we alone together/ among all those   who in the course of time are alone with us/ forming the one choir that murmurs in our shared veins, / our singing veins?* (1968). Also, with Bertolt Brecht's call, "In the dark times/ will there be singing? / Yes, there will be singing / about the dark times" (*Svendborg Poems*, 1938).

The footnote of "Truth and Reconciliation" references an anecdote about Lorca and Dali that I gleaned from Edward Hirsch's *The Demon and the Angel: Searching for the Source of Artistic Inspiration* (Harper Collins, 2003).

SONG OF GRATITUDE:
Opening verse

The seeding and nourishing of art are a community project. This is my humble offering to a global conversation across time and continents. It lives by those who breathe into its essence. Please consider this thanksgiving an opening verse in a song I mean to continue.

This work is made possible by the example of all who have walked the long road, engaged in the beautiful struggle across time and centuries, amid death and encroaching despair—and continued, whose souls were carried by that which was not yet visible, except as it breathed through them.

I dedicate this offering to the vast community that sustains me. To the numerous donors whose endowment afforded my time at The College of the Holy Cross, facilitating my encounters with Bertram Ashe, Christopher Merrill, and Danzy Senna, whose combined influence catalyzed my life's work, and inspired me to find the others. To Coach Jan Mitchell, whose tireless work—on behalf of the thousands of athletes he has coached across decades—made this possible.

To the Ursuline sisters and others who modeled devotion to a life of service learning, whose work prepared me to be a lifelong student of their example—and to the sisters I found while I was with them. To the Mount Miguel community, who have inspired me for two decades and counting—to sing and cry, laugh, and grow, and to stay for far longer than I ever intended, by being such excellent teachers of love. You continue to move me with your heart, your art, your commitment to family, honor, faith, and hope in the dark. To Judy Reeves and the community of San Diego writers and artists who gave me shelter, encouragement, and much needed oxygen at critical times. To the community at San Diego State University, for inspiration and friendship, especially Katie Farris, Hal Jaffe, Stephen-Paul Martin, Yetta Howard, Corrine Goria, Laurie Edson, Bernie Dodge, Jennifer Ruby, Angela Pankosky, Brenda Taulbee, Ryn Corbeil, Libby Stewart, and so many others. To Sandra Alcosser for bringing us together, and to Mary Garcia for making it work.

To those who teach me by their work, including Thomas Merton, Howard Thurman, James Martin; Greg Boyle, Michael B. Curry, Richard Rohr, Krista Tippett, Pádraig Ó Tuama, James Baldwin, David Wojnarowicz, Octavia Butler, Ursula K. Le Guin, Saidiya Hartman, Hortense Spillers, Christian Wiman, Ilya Kaminsky, Jericho Brown, Carl Phillips, Danez Smith, Philip Metres, Adrienne Maree Brown, David Naimon, Lucille Clifton, Jimmy Santiago Baca, Lynn Nottage, Suzan-Lori Parks, Paul Klee, Louise Bourgeois, William Blake, Prince, Clarice Lispector, Marguerite Duras, Carolyn Forché, Edward Hirsch, Willie Cole, Nick Cave, Anne Truitt, Ocean Vuong, Mariama Bâ, Achille Mbembe, Paolo Friere, Cristina Rivera Garza,

Judith Butler, Rebecca Solnit, Courtney Baker, David Lloyd, Bob Marley, Fred Moten, Édouard Glissant; the grandmothers, mothers, sisters, fathers, brothers and others who have held my hands in interfaith prayer and meals and the young people who inspire me daily with their light, laughter, courage, and beats. You return me regularly to the hymn of morning.

To my family, immediate and extended, by whom I am nourished, saved, inspired, relieved, and sheltered—in love, dance, song, faith, and food, even in the darkest hours. I love you.

To Thomas, for your friendship and love. For reading, listening, and seeing me. Anam Cara.

And to Grace, in everything and always.